# THE PORTAGE POETRY SERIES

Series Titles

*The Green Vault Heist*
David Salner

*There is a Corner of Someplace Else*
Camden Michael Jones

*Everything Waits*
Jonathan Graham

*We Are Reckless*
Christy Prahl

*Always a Body*
Molly Fuller

*Bowed As If Laden With Snow*
Megan Wildhood

*Silent Letter*
Gail Hanlon

*New Wilderness*
Jenifer DeBellis

*Fulgurite*
Catherine Kyle

*The Body Is Burden and Delight*
Sharon White

*Bone Country*
Linda Nemec Foster

*Not Just the Fire*
R.B. Simon

*Monarch*
Heather Bourbeau

Praise for
*The Green Vault Heist*

"David Salner's *The Green Vault Heist* combines moments of autobiography, social history, and ekphrasis in a seamless way, and the result is a collection that reveals a compassionate life well-lived. Salner has the power to see into the heart of things, and records the lives of a great range of figures in poems as musical as they are clearly spoken. I dare a reader not to be tempted to read his lines aloud, as they beckon to be heard beyond the page—to feel the pulse and rhythms of the speaker of these poems that are sensitive without fragility, and worldly without cynicism. *The Green Vault Heist* is not only a beautiful book, it is great company."

—John Skoyles
Poetry Editor, *Ploughshares*

"The precision of imagery in David Salner's poetry perceptively offers the past and the present through a 'film of blurred years' to create from the focus of experience works of crisp clarity to be applauded, poems concise yet compelling and ever-celebratory of this life each of us has been given amid 'the quickness of time.'"

—Edward Byrne
Editor, *Valparaiso Poetry Review*

"The poems in *The Green Vault Heist* move the reader through landscapes so clearly described we inhabit them with the writer, at his shoulder, not just seeing and hearing, but tasting 'chopped liver mixed / with eggs boiled hard,' and smelling 'day-old sweat, on night-air / that fills with wine, tobacco, the stale smells of his body. / I breathe that richness / when I need to know I had a father.' The book takes us to baby-boom Baltimore and twenty-first-century Spain and orchestrates those places as the grounds where we live, breathe, and savor our freshly encountered human lives."

—Anne Colwell
Poetry Editor, *The Delmarva Review*

"David Salner's poems sing of the dreams and realities of the working life. In *The Green Vault Heist*, he combines memories of his boyhood in Baltimore and insights from ordinary scenes—looking for a job in Texas, or waiting for a train to pass—with impressions and imagined emotions inspired by music and art, such as Goya's Black Paintings, to further illuminate our humanity. The resulting verse is natural, compelling, compassionate, and memorable."

—David Stephenson
Editor, *Pulsebeat*

"David Salner is a master of his craft with language that is both earthy and visceral yet deeply philosophical. Salner's voice is distinctive whether he is writing about a shoe store or a deli, the natural world or Beethoven's *Eroica*. This is a book not to be quickly read, but to be absorbed."

—Irene Fick
author of *The Wild Side of the Window* and *The Stories We Tell*

"This collection is a quest for knowledge; an ongoing search for essential truths and positive inspirations that creates an informed person who moves through the world. In the final section, we are asked to consider the value of art compared to the perceived trappings of wealth. We are left to question what truly holds meaning and what is a false promise."

—Mark Danowsky
Editor-in-Chief, *ONE ART: a journal of poetry*

"David Salner's works evoke deep and soulful emotion, paintings made of words that are oases of beauty and clarity. We can smell the smoke of his father's cigarettes, and know the cool of the evening air on our skin. He plunges us into the soggy slosh of a rain-drenched day, intimately tying the deluge with an unfiltered longing to escape monotony. Salner's poems are an ode to that ancient longing, belted by singers and chiseled by sculptors, that there must be more to life than this. And in reading his works, we are reminded that perhaps there is."

—Anthony Murphy
Poetry Editor, *Sundial*

# THE
# GREEN
# VAULT
# HEIST

David Salner

Cornerstone Press
*Stevens Point, Wisconsin*

Cornerstone Press, Stevens Point, Wisconsin 54481
Copyright © 2023 David Salner
www.uwsp.edu/cornerstone

Printed in the United States of America by
Point Print and Design Studio, Stevens Point, Wisconsin

Library of Congress Control Number: 2023937896
ISBN: 978-1-960329-06-6

Cover art: "Kitchen Counter Silhouette" © Warren Simons

Cornerstone Press titles are produced in courses and internships offered by the
Department of English at the University of Wisconsin–Stevens Point.

DIRECTOR & PUBLISHER     EXECUTIVE EDITOR
Dr. Ross K. Tangedal       Jeff Snowbarger

SENIOR EDITORS
Lexie Neeley, Monica Swinick, Kala Buttke

PRESS STAFF
Grace Dahl, Zoie Dinehart, Lauren Engelbreth, Brett Hill, Ryan Jensen, Maddy
Mauthe, Brie O'Flyng, Arianna Soto, Chloe Verhelst

*For Barbara, as always*

Also by David Salner:

FICTION
*A Place to Hide*

POETRY
*Summer Words: New & Selected Poems*
*Blue Morning Light*
*The Stillness of Certain Valleys*
*Working Here*
*John Henry's Partner Speaks*

# Contents

## I. Mr. Levitz's X-Ray Machine

## II. A Slack Tide

## III. What Goya Knew

*I project my hat, sit shame-faced, and beg.*
—Walt Whitman

# I.

# Mr. Levitz's X-Ray Machine

# Choice

It's a wonderful thing to have a mother
you didn't come from. I can remember—
when I was four—the heavy varnish on the floor
I was playing on in one of those apartments
built all over Baltimore
after the war. My mother
holds me in the glitter of her black eyes
expressing humor easily, strength and care, and love
with difficulty. She has my father there
for backup. It's a conversation
filled with produce words—"We picked you out,"
as if I were an avocado and they were squeezing
my chubby knees—or a cantaloupe.
My mother sniffs my belly button
while the world looks on. "We'll take this one,"
she announces, "because he's ripe."
Both of them are smoking, and the words
parade in the smoke, dance in the air
high overhead, meaningless as motes

       —for I had already
adopted my mother, when she was a girl
about my age, playing on the marble steps
in a neighborhood where poor Jews lived
in row houses. My orthodox grandmother had a painting
of a handsome man, her husband, who disappeared
when his bank failed. They never saw him again.
As I stared at the painting, I understood
my father would disappear, also,
in a way my mother never would. The words
meant nothing to me, for my mother's eyes
had already told me what I had to know.
I was not the fruit of her body but of something
more important—her choice.
I was the fruit of a woman's choice.

# Mr. Levitz's X-Ray Machine

*By 1970, 33 states had banned*
*shoe-store x-ray machines.*

Mr. Levitz sits on a stool, measuring feet
with a steel slide that feels cool
when it nudges the tip of my toe.
Future and past mean less than the ash

on his cigarette, which will fall on the floor,
because the plate in his head makes him forget
what happened before the war.
But these shoes will fit for a year,

no matter how much I grow,
since my parents don't want to buy new
if they don't have to. He cocks his head
so smoke whispers away from his eyes,

which have a tear in them anyway.
He chats with my mother from a place almost lost
and calls her Rosie, the beauty of Druid Hill,
adds words in Yiddish but forgets

the village in Poland
where uncles and aunts never left.
Mr. Levitz, I always ask, can I look into your machine
at the bones in my feet?

They're green in the rays, green
as the onion dome of the orthodox synagogue
near where Rosie was born.
I laugh and wiggle my toes

while he flirts in a language as dead as the village
his bubby should have left.
But a twinkle survives
between brow and cheek—there—

that small green light that shines
from a bottomless watering trough
and shows us the fiddler, the fire, the ash,
the bones in my little feet.

# Deli with Sea Salt

A world of salt, as seen through the glass
at the butchers counter: meat dripping with fat,
corned beef on veined blocks greasy with
rich white flecks; franks draped in necklaces,

suggestively conic; smoked whitefish;
cream cheese in tubs with pink-orange lox;
wrinkled brown olives in two-gallon vats
filmy with brine; dills in a garlic and vinegar

slosh, each spear still with a pearly white
trace of cucumber left; chopped liver mixed
with eggs boiled hard; only the parched
dough of knishes doesn't taste like it issued

from the sea, where Jonah was swallowed
by the whale, was coughed up and prospered.

# A Boy's Payday

You walk home in the summer heat
from plants near the harbor, along a sluggish Jones-Falls
through hot asphalt vapors, to the markets on Lombard,
where live chickens flap in light blue exhaust,
then duck into Attman's to order a corned beef—
and what could be richer for a Baltimore boy,
than to pay for a corned beef
with his own money?

You wait for your order with surly old men
who cough up their words in an old man's language.
Your eyes drift to the butcher, from his hand to the forearm
flexing on down strokes as he shaves off pink slices
from a slab of fat brisket, to the hairs plastered down
in a light sheen of sweat, to the row
of blue numbers etched into pale skin.

"Enjoy it, kid," he grins,
like he'd been a boy once,
a boy like you, before the tattoo.

# In My Mind's Eye, in Baltimore

on a miserable day to be a child, because of the heat,
how it kept little Bernard, my friend with the bright red hair,
from coming out, along with Jerry and Harold. So, I'm alone

on the back stoop, chin in my hands, with the stink from the harbor—
the shellfish, the waterlogged hawsers—only making it worse,
in that city of crab-feast leftovers, of drab humid mornings—until,

growing louder through heat-shimmer, sounds I can't place,
not urban at all, clop of hooves on macadam, and a voice singing out
to back staircases, "Isaac is here, he needs what you don't."

Mrs. Stark runs down to meet him, gray housedress flying,
with old kitchen items—skillet burned black, cutlery wrapped
in frayed dish towels—which Isaac squints at, offers something,

stuffs it all in his cart, grumbles his thanks, to which she grumbles back,
a gruffness between them, "I need it, you don't," and the cart trundles off
with a hodgepodge worth something to someone.

I sniff at the air, which has cooled since the morning.
Clouds of cinnamon surround me from the mills at the spice plant.
And that night a storm rides up the bay, whips brown water to suds, rocks

small fishing craft, rocks them loose from their bollards. Next morning,
I wake to the rain-chill, hop on my bike, ride to Gwynns Falls
with red-haired Bernard, with Jerry and Harold, streamers flying,

two-wheeling through puddles, screaming all morning. Now,
I'm older than Isaac, than he was then, when he trudged up the alley
over hot macadam, singing out to back staircases—
                                        "Rags and old iron."

# Chain-Link Fence: Bicycle Lesson

I learned to ride on a Baltimore playground
while my father scowled, smoked,
and offered a stream of encouragement
from the distance. Again and again,

I fought for the speed to stay on the pedals.
while he lit another Lucky, impatient
to get back home to his dry martinis.
I practiced, as fireflies filled the schoolyard,

vines sprawled over the chain-link fence,
and weeds, second by second, surged
into Baltimore's humid air. Even now,

I struggle to keep my balance, remembering
that a man stands in his own shadow
offering advice, smoking, doing his best.

## After the Picnic

My mother puts the blanket down,
unwraps wax paper from our sandwiches,
releases the sweet and sour smells
of lunch meat, dill pickles.

My father leans against a tree
with jigsaw bark, drinks something
purple from a glass, shakes another Lucky
from the pack, cups his hands

to light it, sighs the blue smoke
in and out. His eyes meet mine.
I see through them into our future: a job lost,
a long breakdown. After the picnic,

he spirits me into the house
on day-old sweat, on night-air
that fills with wine, tobacco,
the stale smells of his body.

I breathe that richness
when I need to know I had a father.

## Uncle Beale: A Baltimore Boy

He could beat everyone on the public courts
at Druid Hill Park. *Droodle*, it was pronounced. Nearby,
a giant greenhouse, a lake with a dingy fountain.

He served and hit volleys until the Great Depression
bled into a war, which he signed up for. Came home a captain,
kept his silver bars on purple felt.

The bombed-out cities he'd seen in Europe—
Baltimore wasn't like that. Downtown was going crazy;
shoppers hurried through traffic and blue exhaust,

hailed cabs or waited for trollies at Howard and Pratt;
and the mills at McCormick Spice were pumping out
cinnamon, saffron clouds, sweet-smelling

whiffs into a busy port. He wanted to grab a piece
and applied for job after job. But it's useless, he thought,
because of the Jewish name. He had a point, of course,

when you think of the world at that time.
A talented guy, he landed a great-paying job
at a store named for a Mr. Cohen, who had the same

last name he used to have. Don't call him Uncle *Beale*,
Aunt Libby said. Call him Uncle *Ed*.
But we never did.

\*

He tried to return to tennis but ripped a rotator cuff
and had to quit serving, at first, then the overhead smash
where the fun in tennis is at.

He took prednisone just to raise his arm above the waist.
The side-effect was a round face. When I think of my uncle,
it's the eyes I remember most, diamond-bright,

and how he wiped at them with a handkerchief
like he'd been crying or laughing too much.
Like other uncles, he did magic tricks

and knew how to pull a quarter
from behind my ear. It tickled, I laughed.
He dabbed at his eyes with a corner of cloth.

When I was too old for magic, he'd leave a five
as his "donation to the cause." He and Aunt Libby
moved to the suburbs, beyond where Charles Street ends.

I was in high school and mowed their giant lawn, shirt off,
sweating for my "donation." Then I moved away, lost touch,
and heard that he'd joined a church. I went to it once

for the funeral service. When the minister gave the oration,
he left out the Jewish name. Uncle Beale once had a name,
a name and a reason to change it.

# First Check

Fifteen years old. I'm staring at the check,
mesmerized by it, for it's more important
than my own hands, rubbed raw
from swinging a grass whip
through knee-high weeds all week.

I work with Sonny and Mac.
We're dripping with sweat by coffee break.
Sonny gives me the blow-by-blow
for every fight he's ever started.
Mac shows me a handshake with skin.

On Friday, in Baltimore, the eagle flies
through the chrome-colored skies
and the harbor air, freighted with cinnamon
from the grinding machines at McCormick Spice.
All summer long, the heat grinds on,

clouds turn amber from sulfur,
gray from the carbon at Sparrow's Point.
And the eagle flies at the Number Ten stops
and the pawn shops and package stores
full of laughing and crying men.

Laughing and crying, we work until three
and walk back to the office, timing our arrival
for the precise moment when Mr. Obitz,
our pear-shaped boss, has finished the weekly chewing out
and is handing out checks.

I stare at the name of the bank—*Fidelity Something.*
Sonny is dancing and kissing his check.
Mac floats his in the air and snags it
with elegant nonchalance. In my mind's eye,
through urban renewal and rebellion,

we're always receiving those checks.
And in the whole city of Baltimore
*Fidelity Something* no longer exists.

## Four Days at the Point

1.

I drove through the heat and into the grit
of the huge steel mill at Sparrow's Point
but forgot my birth certificate. So I went
home, read *Malcolm X Speaks*, agreed
with him there was no real difference
between the two parties. Next morning,
a shower steamed on the sidewalks,
drenched crab shells spilling from garbage—

2.

and back to the Point, with the paper that
proved I was born at Sinai Hospital, for all
that was worth. Gazed at the burnt roofline,
corrugated walls like a charred washboard,
and flinched from the steel-on-steel shriek
in the air. Then waited in line with broken
and broken-in men, who joked of a life
I hadn't lived yet. We clutched applications
that glossed over our lives, our best lies,
handed them in to a neatly dressed man
who stacked them in careless piles and
hated us just for handing them in. Next day,

3.

as I drove to the Point, the sun rose in a flat
metal sky, a penny afloat in a mist of ash.
And a man in a hard hat gave us
the safety talk, about a worker who slipped

from a catwalk and fell into liquid steel—
I imagined him, his arms would have flapped
as he tried to rise out of the heat, away
from the heat of the Point for a second
of sheer terror as he wondered what it would
feel like to be reduced to a cinder... Back home,
I read Malcolm, again, and knew he was right,
we shouldn't wait for this system to grant us

4.

our human worth. Back at the Point, Day 4,
I waited for hours with half-naked men
just for a doctor to tell me, "These jobs are
for blast furnace work. Sorry, kid, you can't
wear glasses there." So I went back home,
defeated, relieved that I wouldn't be joining
the dead at the Point, not any time soon—
and Dad was out on the porch, half-crocked
on martinis, asking what I'd been up to while
he was at work. "I read *Red Badge of Courage*,"
I lied. If I'd told him I wasted four days at the Point,
he'd have popped in a handful of peanuts
and smirked. Besides, we'd already had one fight
about Malcolm, which was more than enough.

# At the Automat

We walk to the corner of Houston and Second
and stare through the plate glass
at windowed machines, bank after bank of windowed machines
dispensing peach cobbler in identical portions;

turkey on white bread sandwiches;
slices of blueberry pie—the purple is perfect
under a carpet of fluorescent light; and miniature salads
made of lettuce, wisp of tomato,

and julienned carrots—each leaf is identical
when seen through a pane of plexiglass;
and layered cakes arrayed on trays;
and tier upon tier of pudding in goblets.

Look over there, at the line by the cash register,
where a pickpocket chats away
while his fingers explore an army jacket,
divining from the slump and sag, a heavy wallet.

At the next table, skinny dudes, pink noses—this place
is abuzz with crystal-meth dealers and users.
Four cabbies nod over coffee—lost fares, lost fortunes,
discussing the losers and lost

they ferry across the river
to realms of high-rises in the Bronx;
Old-World men, they are the knights
of this up-all-night world.

And the Prince of the tableau
wipes bright yellow custard from a bramble of beard
with the back of his hand. His eyes go shut, go lost,
while he escapes for a sweet hairbreadth

from all the rough stuff of this world, rough stuff
that's real, rougher stuff he imagines.
This must be the place we've been looking for,
this place without atmosphere, where you can eat for a quarter.

## New York

When I lived in New York, I'd bathe in the kitchen
because that's where the bathtub was.
Ancient history. I should keep it to myself.

Some people lead exciting lives,
and who doubts their miraculous stories
of the cave-in, the fire, the flood.

All I can tell you is of the warm bathwater
and the drowsy feel, of looking over the porcelain rim
at a frying pan I didn't get clean.

## Lonely in Philadelphia, 1966

I was lonely in Philadelphia, the city of brotherly love,
so I took off for New York, but ran out of gas in New Jersey,
home of the gas and oil kingdom, and left my '54 Ford
on the road between two refineries. I walked away—
an orange flare shrieked in the grimy air.

No, nothing unusual happened for the rest of February,
and I don't know how many presidents were born in that cold month—
but one day I looked at the newspaper and saw a Buddhist monk
exploding in flames. The fire in the photograph
burned everything but his eyes. They told me to change.

## The Denier

There was a man who denied the grass
under his feet and the birds descending
from the great sky to roost on the graves
and the graves he denied the graves
and no to the skulls of another time
precisely because they were from
another time and no to the smoke
twisting from the stacks and no
to the fire in the furnaces even though
an ember breathed gray and red
beneath a whisper red and gray
and no to the birds he denied
even the grass upon the graves.

Helping My Mother Move In

It's Wednesday, and I've taken the day off work
to help my mother move in
to her new place, where people have forgotten

the "I" in I live here. I bring in a straw basket
and lift out the figurine of an ivory man
and place him on a shelf between two plates.

The dull and lovely pewter of the plates—
they form a bas-relief with the ebony cranes
that stretch their necks into long shrieks.

I put the artificial flowers beside the bed,
and a woman enters in a faded house dress
asking if I've seen two Jewish children.

"I did not abandon them," she swears.
The spring wind
whips sheets of light through the nets of the mind.

It's Wednesday, and I've taken the day off work.
I did not abandon them.
I, of all people …

# Urn

On the day he died, I left
the mourning to my mother.
Poor Mom, there wasn't much
mourning by her, either. Not much
that I could see. No keening, no casket,

no celebration of his life, fond tales and fifths
of single malt. No headstone. Was there an urn?
Were ashes tossed into a breeze that floated him out
to sea? Although, as an Ohio boy, Dad didn't love the sea.
There is no treasured spot that I could visit now, now that I'm

feeling like I should. We scattered Mom's at my sister's house,
which she later sold. The ashes of a friend we scattered at the farm
my daughter moved from not long after. Moved horses, saddles,
blankets, left-over feed, and tack—to a new farm that one day
could become my resting place. And so we move, we all

move on. What I remember—and some was good—
is that he taught me to carry a rifle pointed down
and hold my fists up—but always kick a bully
in the nuts. He tried to teach me the art of
looking down my nose, but that's one

lesson that never took. Although his
DNA survives it's not through
me, the adopted son. I didn't
carry the nucleotide necklace
of his obscure Hungarian line.

Footnote: he had a favorite happy-hour glass,
into which, this afternoon, I pour cheap gin and squeeze a lime.

# II.

# A Slack Tide

## States and Provinces

In Arizona, we camped out
on a trail through the desert
beside the one and only tree.

In Utah, we went down
a northern slope in June
into an inch of snow.

In Idaho, by Hebgen Lake,
a man kept bringing us trout,
fillets the size of my feet.

In West Virginia, we trudged
through the wet shadows
of the mountain rhododendron.

We lay beside the Gulf
which was a *Curacao* blue
in the province of Quintana Roo.

# Clarity

There's a lake I can never find
although I loved it when I was young
and dream of it often. I search in the darkness
surrounding the lake, in the spring-fed forest
of maples, whose great swaying shadows
cool my skin; among clouds of willows
brushing over me, fretful, feathery.

The path I follow in my dream
leads out of this forest, always downhill,
into a region of shoals and hollows, where the air
weighs like a carpet upon my shoulders,
through thickets of leaves and needles,
scrub jungles. I hold up my hands
to shelter my face from the slap of green branches.

Then the undergrowth disappears
and a cool breeze stirs. My bare feet discover
coarse sand, a few pebbles. I hear the waves,
small and ceaseless, as they radiate
in circles around the shoreline. I kneel
and dip my hand in the lake and hold
the ice-cold water in my mind.

# A Radiance

*for Lily and Paul*

The morning light
blows in gusts through lowered blinds.
Beyond the guest room, Paul is letting the horses out
into their weedy paddock, lifting the two by four—
dry wood wheezing in an iron latch. Then I lie back
and listen to the bees, alerted by the rising sun,
singing in gold forsythias; a carpenter
goes to work, the saw
squealing its caustic message to the grain
then dying out; and in its place, cicadas
sing in the ruffling trees, signaling
the heat of another summer day. I roll over,
hear Lily's voice, scolding and sweet,
calling from the porch—*come, you dear bad dog!*
The clink of chinaware on granite tells me
that in the kitchen far below, a cup of coffee
waits. I hug them both,
go out into a haze of sun on gravel, pull down the visor,
drive east. One stop for gas
and then the bridge. Sunlight through iron beams
and brine-soaked cables. A radiance
across the endless lapping of the Bay.

Savannah Channel

A shrimper drifts by
trailing nets through the water
with a drag on the stern, heavy and quiet.

He turns away from the sun,
the bright steel of morning,
bends over his shadow, intent on a ticklish repair

or so I imagine.

Gulls, pelicans, and a mysterious bird
that dives under water and searches for fish,
all follow the chug, the small wake of the engine.

The tide goes out,
the beach is littered with nettles.
Night comes on, a landward breeze over brackish waters.

And the shrimper returns,
a speck on the smoke-colored tide, a ghost, leaving only
the soft, dark notes of the engine.

## Around Phelps Lake

Pontoons shift with each step, waver
beneath us. We walk around a lake
bristling with cypress. Small waves
lap over pink roots, pink in the sun,
pink as skinned knuckles. We unfold
chairs in the wind. Small boats rock
on swells, mooring lines creak,
fibers grow taut around iron bollards.
A yellow butterfly dodges among
purple wildflowers; a dragonfly
whips the air to a shimmer, rattles
dry stalks; the sun is an insight,
an opal in gray. You leap up,
set the hook on a catfish,
and soon you have five,
tails waving, treading dreamily
on a green stringer gleaming
through glassy water. I take them
to the campsite, sock each
with a dead-blow hammer, spike
tails to a sweet gum tree, tug
at the skin, slip knife up the side,
shave meat from the white spine bones.
Clouds scatter. A slant of afternoon sun
catches the smoke from our fire.
We wrap them in foil, drop parcels
on coals sighing red, sit back,
and gaze through a collar of spruce,
boughs lit by fire, a halo of white
feathers against the night sky. We peel
blackened foil like a crisp skin,
suck at the flaky meat, pump up

the fire with kindling to hold off
black bears and whatever footloose
spirits might frequent these fens. I finish
my second beer, all I'm allowed,
as the air cools, breathes over sweat.
And think of you leaping up
from the dock, setting the hook.

## At Swallow Falls

It took some climbing to perch on that rock above the rapids surrounded by sound, the roaring magnified among mountains in a stillness of green-black spruce.

I crawl to the edge, belly on sandstone, stare twenty feet down to a pool, a miracle of disappearance and darkness and depth with white water seething around.

I study the falls while you catch the day's only fish, a small sunny, unlock the barb from the soft bone jaw, let it fall to the pool with a plink. The surface heals over the sound.

Boulders surround us, totems shaped by an ancient sea then left a moment. One day they'll dislodge and wash from these shoals into an age of peace.

Above the far slope, a beam of sun in a haze of campfire smoke. I've lain on this boulder long enough, feeling how small a man can be, an anxious man among deafening waters.

We hike back the uphill trail, I get winded, stop to rest on a fallen tree, then coax myself on through needles and leaves. We climb from the forest and catch the heartrending call.

Two hikers are coming behind us, and before they emerge from the trailhead, we know what they're crying for. The shape and feel of each word breaks over the sound of the falls.

## Recalling Texas Rivers

A ten-dollar bill burns in the tank
as I curve around Canyon Lake, an hour north of San Antonio,
then swing south on 281, across the Guadalupe, a tiny river
stuffed with white water—asking where is it best to be unemployed,
in New York or Heaven? Or here in Texas,

where overnight storms have buried the banks of the Frio,
full of icy fish; and the Comal, known as the Turquoise Jewel,
the shortest river in the world. I check the mailbox for scorpions
and an unemployment check from New York. One would poison me,
the other feed me, but nada.

A bottle of cheap tequila sits by the keyboard, with a lemon,
that righteous, yellow fruit. I sprawl on my mattress as afternoon shadows
play over the wall. Outside the house, leaves rustle, an armadillo
rummages in a patch of bugleweed. Those rivers are quiet now,
debris washed clear in the surge.

And deep in the earth, a pure-water clamor
echoes in limestone caverns.

## Slack Tide, Massey's Landing

Below me, around the pilings, in brine-slaked air
so thick I taste the salt, in gray fog,
as I luff clumsily between the grays of sky and bay—
the inlet streams with all the strength of seven seas,
tugs at my two-ounce sinker as I loosen line.
A gust across the Landing almost takes my hat
and my line goes slack.

The troubled seas that rule the inlet all relent,
as if a hand upon the water calmed the depths,
the haul and tow of it. I lay my rod upon the railing,
rest elbows on the wood, pitted by years of rain, wind-kerfed.
A cormorant stalls overhead, a charcoal smudge
upon a leaden sky, surveying the length and breadth
of this new stillness, searching for movement
in the silence, a hint would be a feast.

The lull persists, reminding me
of when I lie beside my wife, and she
has just breathed out—I listen as each second
swells into the slow time of the universe—
then finally her breath again.

And to think of all that must be happening
in this moment, from Winnipeg to Singapore
but not here, where the flow of time
has ceased to buffet me, this angler in a trance
above it all, above the laughter of the world,
laughter and horror, in a spell cast by the moon.

Then, movement, something twitches
in a marsh across the inlet, a heron nods, lifts
a leg stiff as a stalk, scans the shallows,
where the surface seems to dance with hidden
tension, ripple with an underlying force—

I sense the pressure all around me, swelling
until the channel brims and flows
and the new tide is on us.

## Where Shells Come From

Periwinkle, clam, or whelk—
like stones, these sea-worn shells.
All colors buffed away, an ivory sheen is left,
perhaps a whisper of purple across the upturned belly, purple
like the inside of the sea, looking upward through the waves—
if you were drowning, what you would see.

\*

Once, these shells protected sea-blood, flesh.
Not sure what kind of life that was, what kind of holding
shells could give. But now a constant surf has broken,
beaten and blended them
to seamless seasoned stone.

\*

Real stones are heavier, wash lower in the surf.
Not like these whitened flakes, helpless as gull's feathers,
fathoming a way to happen here, so far from Africa,
where shells come from.

\*

Our true home was never here, this sandy strip—
but in the sea, a sea of risk, that pure smooth
tumult pushing and sucking us, where we first learn
to clutch at water, cling to liquid, float,
then glimpse the sun through waves—
rays lapping and flowing overhead—
as the wonder of our lives floats off.

## Night Train

The fields disappear
into the darkness beyond the tracks
as you listen to the clack-clack-clack
from the weight of the wheels bearing down
over miles of cross-ties and wonder
for no reason whatsoever what if
you could step down when it slows
for a crossing and become someone else
the man in that truck waiting by the tracks
gripping the wheel feeling
the heavy vibration at the engine's heart
and the miss that makes it stumble almost stall
until you rev it and a plume of exhaust
turns pink in the crossing lights. Could smoke
because what else would you do while you
wait for this long train to pass. Could breathe
a song of smoke into the country night
as you watch for the arm of the gate to swing up
and the road ahead to clear. Could follow
the center line as it unwinds between fields
into a forest where the tar of the two-lane
changes to gravel and the truck stops in a clearing
filled with the smell of pine needles
fallen on loam and the call and call again
of tree frogs through the window
the vibrant swell the pulse of their longing. Could wait
at the heart of that circle of trees where the air
has been washed by a shower that day
clean of judgment and knowing. Could walk
the stone steps to the porch
and turn the knob and feel how easily
the door swings open into a hallway

where someone is standing so close in the darkness
you feel her sigh on your cheek. Could breathe
that one word *want* one syllable
that would guide you through the night
and into a new life. Could step down
at this crossing and wait by the tracks
for this long train to pass.

# Steam

At any given moment,
our minds fill with visitors
seen through a film of blurred
years, flimsy and restless shapes
arriving when we should have been
doing who knows what—and does it
matter to anyone but you how she
stepped from a steamy shower,
ratted her hair with a towel,
and disappeared?

# The Celebration

*for John and Mabel*

Music and laughter as I enter
his parents' house, cradling
a fifth of *Chivas*, placing it
beside an ice-blue bottle of *Bombay*,
a jewel-smooth *Absolut*—
                just so,
these lovely bottles, the glasses,
the bucket filled with ice—
                just so,
we enter this hubbub to escape
the clarity of tomorrow.
                Today,
in the chill mountain air,
we heard the soft unwinding
of the ribbons of grief
on which the casket rests, the silent
gears releasing on a winter day
the weight of a boy to gravity,
into the hours of the earth.
                Above us,
above the streams he fished,
above the forest trails he skied,
compacted to a diamond hardness—
the stars sing to a skyline
of the dark and mute Uintas.
Above a wilderness of feeling.

# Without St. George

The tyrant Dacian stretched St. George
on the rack then pressed him in a box
through which nails were driven; salted his wounds
with hair cloth; dunked him in boiling water.
And that was not the end of his torture.

We have no saints today, no one like that,
but there is one ordinary prisoner named Gerardo,
who was held in isolation seventeen months,
seventeen months in his underwear,
without a blanket, without a window.

For seventeen months with the lights kept on
so he couldn't sleep or tell day from night.

The days of St. George and his courage
have long since passed. Our lives go on without him.
I would not compare the two men.
But you can write to Gerardo at Victorville Prison
in California—and he will write back.

## No One Asks

Beyond doubt's shadow, his face stares back,
    flattened and fish-like and mugshot dull,
a scowl without a dream. Is he still alive
    after twenty years of appeals denied?

His photo stares back—an absent grin,
    a bruise, a scar—beside a one-column article:
*Governor Mulls Prisoner's Plea.* Hard to imagine
    life behind that shadowed face.

Perhaps you have a brother you haven't seen
    for a while, with an absent grin—
but that's not him, not the same face, not him.
    No one asks you to imagine it is.

# For Leonard Peltier

I sat down to read about Crazy Horse,
but the books told me little
except that he gave everything to the poor
and loved Black Buffalo Woman.

No one alive is like him.
But there is one man
who has spent most of his life in prison.
From this man, I could learn about Crazy Horse.

## Plant

From the blacktop road
and the school bus stop
look down the lane
between muddy pastures
and wire cow fences
to that house
where a man
who'd like to be
feeding the world
raises his hands
to plant the barrel
of a shotgun in his mouth...

# Their World

In the world of the dead
the sun sets every morning;

the pious pray to shadows
they call light;

the successful live in a prison
of their success;

the rich live long lives
in the comfort of their self-love.

And the Arbiter,
who lives to correct everyone else?

Like a stopped clock,
twice a day he's correct.

Twice.
At most…

# That Kind of Rain

*For Echol Cole and Robert Walker**

It rained that day,
that kind of rain
when puddles rattle all day long
with drops that sting like buckshot;
when tires slick by,
        kick spray into your face;
when all the cans in shabby alleys
overflow with trash so wet
        it dissolves each time
you try to pick it up; when all the news
in papers blown down avenues
        where rich folk live
is bad. The kind that presses you
to almost give up hope that maybe
        once this afternoon
the sun will shine in woods,
a breeze will sing in words
and thoughtful sentences,
        and each new day will hold
more than a foothold
on a speeding truck, more than
a search for shelter from the rain.

---

*Sanitation workers killed in their truck on February 1, 1968, prompting a strike and the visit by Martin Luther King to Memphis.

# Old Soldier, Lower East Side

*For G. J.*

*RikkaRikk*—the wind

rattled in airshaft windows fifty years ago
when you put Doc and Merle on the RCA
and their flat-pick guitar and country tenors
soared throughout the Lower East Side,
from Tompkins Square to Second Ave.,
above the grated, midnight shops—

then the brakeman yodeled his "Mule Skinner Blues"
across the tar rooftops of tenements—
as two poor boys donned their best slum-elegance,
downing extra-dry, pure-gin martinis,
while Lefty, Hank, and Patsy
warbled blues and jubilation to the night.

**

You fought *in* and fought *against*
slaughters falsely called your service, and in that fighting
earned yourself a ride upon the "good road,"
as Jimmie called it. So when the water boy
sets down his bucket, lift the ladle and drink up.
You might just find an olive in it.

# An Old Man Who Believed in Math

Archimedes works by the breakers, writing formulas in the sand
He stands back to admire his work, as the surf comes in from Africa
wave after wave, swirling around his ankles.

A Roman soldier interrupts this scene as if he, also, has something to prove.
"In the name of The Empire—erase those formulas!"
The old man refuses. "Only the sea can erase my formulas."

So the soldier buries his sword in the mathematician
and feels much better, triumphal, even,
for serving The Indispensable Nation.

Centuries pass, and the Empire crumbles. It was more of a herald
than cause and effect. But still, an old man who believed in math
defied a Roman soldier on the beach.

# Your Fugitive Life

A truck zooms by, the sound of the engine
rising, then falling into the distance
of your long-lost life. Will you wake up
back in the windowless cell, alone and without
wife or girlfriend to visit you? Or in a new life,
the old name, the old trademarks and labels
washed off, the crud of a lifetime scrubbed clean
by the breathtaking rush of your escape?

\*


Learn how to hide in plain sight. First of all,
discard old habits, which mark you as sure as a fingerprint.
Throw them off track by visiting museums instead of old haunts

like pool hall and dog track; on Sundays, read the *Times* in a coffee shop.
Your new name, your alias, will work fine, but put flesh on the bones
by borrowing facts from people you've known. Like Groundhog,

your friend with the nickname—steal a few items from his identity,
the painful divorce and the daughters he never sees
because of that stupid argument with his wife. You don't need to say

what it was about, just mutter under your breath when the topic comes up.
And remember they're *your* daughters, she's still *your* wife.
But the nickname—that would stand out. Besides,

you're not really a "groundhog," no rounded shoulders,
no eye tooth. Disguise and invent, mix colors like a painter, but always
blend in. A good tip: carry a keyring wherever you go, although

you don't own a car or home, not even a lock
for toolbox or bike. Keep your lies straight. Smile forthrightly
as if you have nothing to hide, especially when you chat up

a boss or a cop. You'll have to work under the table, which means
no checks from welfare or unemployment. Or Social Security,
which wouldn't amount to much anyway. No driver's license,

no image of your face, which looks quite distinguished
with bifocals, which now that you're older you can't read without,
and the new salt-and-pepper beard. Give it some gusto. It's almost fun

once you've learned to lie to yourself. Still, it might hurt
not to see those daughters. By now, the oldest is grown.

# Ore Train, Early Morning

The arm with the flashing red light comes down,
and who doesn't enjoy a train speeding by
with the clack of the wheels and the *tat-tat-*

*tat* of the burnished rails slapping down
on creosote ties in the post-dawn chill?
Quite a sight, too, as I think of it now,

forty years on, how the mist shimmers off,
mothlike, from hot ore pellets bedded high
in rust-brown cars. A moment to fight for

as the name speeds by, *DMIRR, DMIRR*
a song of steel rushing out of the dark,
holding me while a moment draws out

that could last forever, for all I cared then,
for all I care now. Then a hard winter sun
stirs up the wind, the first of the morning,

whips snow over ballast and cinders,
moans in the curve and sway of the spruce—
and the train disappears on its way to Duluth.

## The Royal, the Whiskey, the Snow

I'd been drinking and punching keys on my
Royal clackey-clack, while snow was falling
on hedges and hoods, making even the trash
in the cans look beautiful outside the shack
I lived in. And that was years ago.

All sound was muffled but the crunch of tires
compacting snow, and the ding of the carriage return.
Earlier, I'd cleaned the keys with a safety pin,
prying the blue-black clots from the bellies
of the b's and o's. And that was years ago.

I got up to shovel so that the next morning
when most of the valley was still asleep
I could enter the great cold stillness and drive
to a power plant where the wind shrieked
around towers and stacks. And that was years ago.

When I came back to my shot glass
from shoveling steps and salting the path,
the windows were coated with a haze of breath
frozen from head to sash—and I wondered if this
was the last poem I'd write. And that was years ago,

long before Dell and Microsoft. I was happy
and desolate and treasured the feeling
I was alone in the world and destined for nothing
but that present tense of bourbon and snow,
very soon to change. And that was years ago.

# Leave Me a List

Withdrew our stocks
from the IRA

so we can pay
our credit card debt.

Let the market sink
to its heart's content.

Decided
to hold the gold.

Before you leave for work
get what you want

from the freezer, maybe
the last of the rockfish.

Next summer
we'll catch some more.

I'll go shopping
for wine and milk and

whatever else we need.
Leave me a list.

## Blue Grass Poem

You were spilling your guts out, as usual,
as we drove into the Blue Grass State
from the West Virginia side, looking for work.

We wanted to pick up on the rumors,
so we stopped for some fast food,
and they told us one steel mill was running

but the other one was down, and a lot
of folks would have trouble this Christmas.
I checked the want ads while you talked,

and we went back through the parking lot,
hands in pockets, shoulders bumping, you talking,
and the traffic fell on your voice like earth.

I could see what you were saying, only too late.
And then we left the Blue Grass State.

# A Meditation on the Land

*—remembering a farm foreclosure.*

*For Darrell Ringer, 1953–93*

"Thank you," he said, while the black eyes
drilled from the shadow of his ballcap
as we stood in the sunbaked square
of a Kansas town where we'd just rallied
against such business as no one with honor
should dare to defend—then drove
over pocked macadam, between shoulders
cascading with purple wildflowers, wheat
turning green to gold—the field after field,
the rich carpet called forth, turned over,
culled with such care that I, for one,
don't have blisters enough to imagine—
and beneath it the black earth seethes
with world-feeding life. Then we arrived
at his farm. Beautiful, I'd often thought,
this life, how the green soybean hug
at the earth and alfalfa explodes into pink
and animals trudge toward us in the slow-
motion rhythm of paddock-bound shadows
until their heads hike up with quick interest
when hay bales are pitched with a thud
between the tarnished steel rails of the crib.
But the earth and its moods are uncertain,
despite the disconsolate pleading it gets
when sleep doesn't come, that a storm
please pass by without flooding at harvest;
that a drought not set in, the wind not whisk
topsoil to a powder-dry ash floating off
in a glitter-filled cloud to the red
of a summer-long sun. And of course

words are addressed to the Notice of Debt
that's attached like a leech to the title,
which is after all a mere sheet of paper
approved by the courts but without
the least smell of wet dirt to grace it.
And of all he foresaw or was faced with,
what he couldn't agree to was losing this land
without even a fight. They might take it all,
but the fight, at least—they couldn't take that.

## Ghost Town Nocturne

We knew we'd never return.
Before the weeds grew tall, we knew,

before the rich dirt buried the town, we knew.
Buried all who once lived there, including two lovers

who always came late for work, because to the question
what lends meaning to life—work or love—they'd already

arrived at an answer, and it was compelling. And this meaning,
which they embraced so tight they could feel its heartbeat—

this meaning—its cadence and flood—they meant to preserve
like a fruit in the sweetness of time. And afterwards, the sigh,

not so much for a moment lost forever but for its fullness.
And their total absorption in each other, the baffling minutes

afterwards when they stared amazed, asking almost in unison,
*what are you thinking—a penny for your thoughts.* One moment,

sly teenagers, too knowing to admit to any such wonder, the next,
die-hard believers in love. Until their cell phones screamed out

*hurry for work!* Which required no small sense of purpose
and great strength for the toilsome moment of tearing-away.

But making it on time was not really of lasting concern,
since his workplace first, then hers, went out of business

when the roll-downs slammed hard and fast to the tarmac.
Then a silence in which you could have heard a pin if it

dropped in a tub of curdled milk forgotten on a sideboard
while the town emptied out. And if you went back now—

and I say *you* because *I* never will—you might find a lonely street
and a ramshackle porch where you could listen for that one

moment, the precise musical measure that flickers like the light of a star
from a long way off, like a sound you can hear, barely, before it's lost—

from the beginning of time or the end of it. Or from the instant
two lovers shared as they surged in the quickness of time.

# III.

## What Goya Knew

# The Black Paintings

*Museo del Prado, Madrid, 2015*

## 1. A Room in the Prado

We were glad to escape the late morning sun
off the alabaster walls, and to enter the Prado
and feel cool air in the high-ceilinged rooms—
and as our eyes got used to the play of shadow,
the first colors we saw were of waterlogged wood,
in Sorolla's large canvas, and the faded blue
on a water barrel. And the tenderness
of the two fishermen, kneeling in the hull,
arching over them like a chapel, as they
cradle their sea-brother. They lower his head,
now a cold stone, to the floor, where the sea
still pulses. Then rise to trim sails and secure
a poor catch to pay for the funeral. How small
we are, how large our tenderness to each other.

## 2. Goya's Black Paintings, Melville's White Whale

Melville looked out and beheld a pale horse
and from that derived the idea that white,
the absence of color, is more horrifying to us
than black. He had his own reasons. But if alive today,
he might have listed the white sun beating down
on cities—bombed-out, no drinking water—or the milky froth
on the waves overwhelming a crowded ferry. We are there—
feel the surf on the trembling hull, as we await a white

vortex that will suck us like jettisoned luggage
down to a final refuge. We implore the one nation—
shining in its ghostly correctness—to resolve
our refugee status. But how long should we wait
for a capsizing nation? Oh Goya, is the blackness you painted
more frightening than the white storm we live in?

### 3. Two Old People Starving

—based on Goya's *Two Old People Eating*

I am that crone
wanting to eat
and the spoon
in my hand
glows like a scepter
and my partner
is a parcel of bones
stacked on the table
and both of us point
appealing to someone
beyond the dark frame
to solve the dilemma
of the first morsel
who should get it

## 4. What Goya Knew

That some men think they are graceful, proud of the wrist-flick
that lops off a head; that a woman who appears to be doing laundry
is snipping the thread of life; that nations boast men so fierce
they can tear off a child's head with their teeth;

that our pilgrimage is led by a fat priest on a horse
that wobbles as it treads the long path; that the saints who watch over us
report back to the devil; that liberation cannot be forced on us
by a bayonet but must be defended by one, at all cost;

that all knowledge was first whispered by outlaws
then written down in forbidden books; that holy men
who preach gentleness would have us bow before beasts;

that those you thought were tougher than nails
will die this winter; that the night air is only cold
on the skin of those who are frightened by death.

## Van Gogh: Wheatfield and Starry Night

If I hold the harvest, I will not go mad
       to reap the vision of my wheat, just scythed
    and waving in a field of yellow stalks

         blown by a wind that raves inside my head,
scatters my thoughts, once in a neat sheaf tied,
      now by the fury of a mental storm unleashed

   into a sky of black crows' wings that beat
       blue air into a storm of rage and loss.
If I hold the harvest, I'll see things as they are

    with square bales squarely on the ground.
       Not in this landscape where a frightened town
huddles beneath a cypress and a spire,

    awed by a dozen haloes in the sky
       and the vortex of a wild careening star.

## L'amante Impaziente

Beethoven composed *L'amante impaziente*
to a lyric by Trepassi, a lesser court poet,
which means he had to put up with—*my,*
*that was gorgeous; darling, I couldn't*
*agree more with*... a superfluity
from the rich and famous in exchange
for a place at a truly 'magical' table
including starpower, a few snide jokes,
and a dessert of buttery biscuits topped
with sweet lemon drizzle, or Florentines
in dark Perugian chocolate, take your pick
or enjoy it all. But let's leave aside
the court and its favors; the dubious merit
of the rich and famous; not to mention
that Beethoven himself for all we know
was in love with Florentines—leave all
that aside and listen to the music as it
strives for rich notes of longing, a cadence
of frustrated yearning. For aren't we all—
poets, artists, musicians, workers of every
stripe and persuasion—aren't we all
lovers? aren't we all impatient?

# The Baptism of Christ in the Crowded Uffizi

This *Baptism* offers a welcome relief
from the sun on the rooftop café
where I go to relax but keep glancing around
at the line of people waiting for me
to finish my beer and overpriced scone.
                    And to my eye, at least,
the Jordan River looks more like a tarn, which is fine—
who among us wouldn't love to stand there, cooling our feet
in a crystal pool, naked in the mountain air?
                    And here's the thing—
the water in the tarn is invisible, it's so clear,
except for the tracery of a delicate line
around the ankles of the Son of Man.
                    And what a relief
that Leonardo has washed out the torture and pain
Bosch or Bruegel would have put in this scene:
                    a row of scaffolds
etching a threat across the skyline; serrated blades
behind hayricks or glinting from shadows; hell fires
flaring from holes in a churchyard.
                    And in this *Baptism*
there's a charming nonchalance to the angel-children,
who gaze from a rocky shelf at the king of kings
with the realistic whiskers and the ringlets
drenched by water from a silver bowl
held high by John.
                    This water, also, is invisible
or nearly so, much like when the sun
highlights a shower on the horizon
and you feel the rain cleansing the earth,
washing the air to a crystalline moment
when nature, like art, is almost perfect.

# A Painter in 18 Lines

*for Eddy Canellos*

I know nothing about her life, except
for three paintings on my living room wall. Well,
I did ride in a sports car with Curt, her husband,
who had a patch on one eye. Also,

Curt and Eddy fled Austria after the war.
Bad things happened after the war,
as well as before and during. Once,
she took me into a field to paint horses,

red and brown, bending muzzles to earth,
tearing huge tufts of grass. And today
she is unknown. Would that surprise her,
or would she tell me: No,

the years after Curt's death were long.
I hardly remember them myself.
But what a surprise!
A little boy remembers that day

we painted horses in a spring field.
Or cares enough to imagine he does.

# Questions from the Museo Fran Daurel

*Barcelona, September 5, 2015*

Why is the patient one the gray baboon?
Why is the fabric of mutation made of steel?
Why does a solitary leg march down the road?
Why does the heart expel a crowded boat?

Why does the light bulb hang above the lamb?
Why do their mouths speak only words of foam?
Why does the man put on an empty suit?
Why does the heart expel a crowded boat?

Why does a scream hide in a clamshell ear?
Why did she vanish, the girl into the wind?
Why does the Blue Division sit upon a throne?
Why does the heart expel a crowded boat?

Why are two yellow dabs of egg left in a pan?
Why does the dog swim through a pool of blood?
Why do the ashes float out of the hat?
Why does the heart expel a crowded boat?

# Loss—and the Green Vault Heist

*On Nov. 25, 2019, thieves broke into the renowned*
*Dresden museum, the Green Vault, pulling off*
*history's richest museum heist.*

## 1.

The security cameras were on, but all they show
is black trousers and the glow

of flashlights roaming a checkerboard floor and the *scuffle scuffle*
of thieves packing a sack with a sword, a shoe buckle,

and hat clasp, all studded with diamonds—the haul of it!
Not to mention the diamond-encrusted epaulet!

And a 49-karat diamond ring belonging to a beautiful woman.
You'll see her in royal portraits somewhere: porcelain

cheeks to go with a discombobulation in her eyes, which some say was coy.
No doubt, she treasured this generous toy,

though gems are far too often given
not so much to commemorate beautiful women

as to keep them chained. Not pretty, in point of fact,
the untold stories of these jewels, which survived intact

the Allied bombing of Dresden. Which most humans didn't.
Diamonds are hard, flesh isn't.

## 2.

That's all you need to know about diamonds, unless you've got bitcoins enough to place a bid, access to the right address on the dark web—and the nerve to go there.

What else resides in the Green Vault? Well, I visited once, as a lowly tourist, and this former residence of the Saxon Kingdom was full of the baubles and junk you find in most royal palaces, though one room held vitrines that I studied so long I almost missed the tour bus. There, on green felt, the real treasures nestled, ivory figures with paper-white, swan-like necks, turned on a lathe by *turners*, they were called.

And just as seamlessly as a gloved hand snatches a gem into a dark corner of the universe, let us transport ourselves back several centuries to the turner, hovering over the spinning ivory, out of which he'll create the stems connecting a universe of glowing orbs in a gossamer network, world upon glossy world, his duty to create. He's only dimly aware of a tired foot on the treadle, and the sharp looks of his boss, a know-nothing royal.

The rough shaft spins as he slides the steel tool along its length, shaving a fraction off in each pass, just so, without pitting or cracking the piece. Under this nibbling caress, the piece on the lathe dwindles to a delicate spindle, which he hones with an emery cloth.

Then for a silky finish, he eases his foot off the treadle and lets the ivory spin from inertia and takes a soft rag and cossets the piece till it glows in the center of a dark room full of a bright snowfall of ivory dust.

Now he's got a moment, at most, to enjoy his creation as the spinning piece slows then comes to rest, radiant in the warm candlelight.

Then back to work, making wheel spokes for a carriage because his young lord insists on whipping the horses' rumps over bumpy lanes and highway ruts.

3.

Apparently the diamonds could not be insured for a set price
since they'd been appraised as "priceless." Ah, the subtle
valuations that robbed the museum twice.

But is nothing in art truly priceless?
I'm thinking of Ellen's Third Song, the music
by which Ave Maria is known to us,

composed by an Austrian I would compare
to that ivory turner—although music exists
in time not space, pure notes in the air.

He died of typhoid at age thirty-one
and suffered with VD his whole adult life.
What if somehow those thieves had stolen

Ava Maria to a dark-web place
where only bitcoin-cutthroats could enjoy it?
Life would continue for us in all the same ways

but without the same possibility
to feel that much pain
and find it lovely.

# Leaving Spain

*for the memory of R. G.*

Headed for the Alicante station
on a stretch of EU highway no one drives,
we open the lunch bag packed by Eva
containing slices of sesame rye,
olives, chunks of *queso manchego*,
almonds, an *empanada*, still warm.

Our train stops in Valencia, accelerates
through orange groves, past irrigation trenches.
Each holds a narrow gloss of water,
mirrors a fragment of the sky.
Blocks of quartz stacked by the tracks
shatter sunlight into green, translucent shards.

From before we left, the image of a lizard
streaks across the shoulder of the pool
and leaves a blur upon the sunbaked day,
a hazel stain on alabaster. Surrounded by cactus,
high above the seaside calamari stands,
stucco walls trace sharpened pencil lines

against a perfect blue, a depth of sky. In this land,
all things are marked by demarcation, the clash
of elements at their edges. But in the stucco house—
darkness. Robert will sleep all afternoon,
or try to. Wake from a double-dose—
chemo, radiation—gulp the air he needs

to entertain his friends with talk
about events in Barcelona, about the red and yellow
ribbons of *Valle de los Caídos*, where the tyrant

lies buried, will not always be. His face lights
to an hour's conversation for words
are the reward for what he lives through,

a run of words he chisels into time, our lasting stone.
Surrounded by parched olive groves
and ragged rows of pomegranate, we talk
past sundown, when a soft breeze comes to us
flowing from a range of bluffs down to the sea,
a gray mirage below a gauzy sky.

We watch a spume climb from the waves
into a haze, an opal mix with no horizon line.
No past or future. The present is a veil of clouds,
an envelope for hearts to beat within.
Twilight. In the corner of an eye,
the pain leaks back.

*


We are prepared to tiptoe from the house
and let him sleep, but he wakes in the afternoon
and follows us to where the sun beats down
upon the cobbles. With Eva bracing him,
he stands before a purple bougainvillea,
grins into the future, waves.

# Eroica, 2022

I love how the bows
mow over their catgut strings,

how each time they pierce the air
in unison the moaning becomes a cry

filling the hall, a draw and thrust based on
trust in the measures and the nervous dance,

the sudden stabs the conductor makes; and I'm
enthralled by the orange-brown glow of rosewood,

surprised by the throaty roar of an ocean of strings
as they rally against the heartbreaking breakdowns,

the upending ups and downs of the hard-pressed folk
of Beethoven's time; and how fast we leap to applaud

this music, which is now more than two centuries old!
After an intermission for pinot noir, seltzer, over-priced

beer, we're back in the hall, *bravoing* our conductor,
who tells us the orchestra just signed a union contract

after a lock-out lasting six months! Nor was it easy,
I imagine, for the strings to sit idle so long; then

our *Eroica* resumes, when three golden horns
proclaim a chorus of Down with All Kings.

# Powder Blue Cadillac
*—Hank Williams, Jan. 1, 1953*

If we're born into our death, each of us,
then he was born into the need to drink
himself to death. Which he was doing
on this last ride, when he told the driver
who was 17, to stop at the convenience store
for a pint of whiskey and a twelve-pack
*son of a gun, we'll have some fun.* That done,
he started in on small talk, asking if the boy
liked the new song, "Jambalaya," just now
peaking on the charts. It's not my favorite,
he answered him. That's because you don't
know French, the singer laughed, the man
who didn't have that much to laugh about.
Then both of them shut up as sleet began
to fly in whiteout sheets across the road.
They took a break in Charleston, but when
they started up again, the sleet was worse.
The driver sensed that something wasn't
right about the silence *oh me oh my oh,*
so he pulled off at the Oak Hill hospital
for a doctor to come out and poke the man
who knew such pain, such pain as we all
feel but shouldn't have to, sprawled out
across the back seat. Can't you revive him,
can't you do something, he cried, the child
in all of us *crawfish pie and filé gumbo.* No,
he's dead, the doctor said, just dead. Which
was true, as far as it went, although the doctor
might have tried a few words more to ease
the pain, unless he felt that after all we've
seen *ma cher ami-o* and what's ahead of us,
words are suspect, not worth a lot as balm.

# Falling

Beyond the plate glass of this thrift store
a pelt of rain drifts off down the coast
leaving puddles that shimmer on hot asphalt

beneath a sunset of meandering clouds
over rooftops. I try on a pair of dress shoes,
a comfort to wear, even after the toes curl up

and heels wear down on one side, so I'd fall
into you as we walk. What's walking, Twain said,
but a fall that you catch. And maybe a hand

to cradle an old man's elbow, a nest after flight,
and an offer to guide him back to his house.
A fall with a catch and a gasp that we hide,

like the glimpse of a death we all know
but know not much about. All I know is my falling
for you led to year after year of falls into you.

And the dress shoes I made up my mind to buy
are like new when daubed with a peppery polish
and brushed to a shine by a good flannel cloth.

## The View from Heaven

where the floors are made of a glass so clear
when I stare through them I seem to float, and it's breathtaking
and dizzying to hover like this, as on the top floor of a skyscraper,

looking into the dark cleft between buildings, slipping into the shadows
where everything seems to be happening, where the walls pulse with music, throb
like the chambers of a child's heart, and the streets fill with drunks and flowers,

and the nights are alive with voices that brawl with anger or whisper
hurt phrases of longing, and throaty laughter beckons the lively
through a network of tracts and hidden arteries, and there

in the depths by a flight of stone steps where I left it,
my soulful artifact, which lends meaning
to everything I can never have back.

# Epilogue

According to news released by the German authorities in December 2022, the police had recovered 31 items from the 2019 Green Vault heist. Among these are a diamond-encrusted breast star and a richly jeweled heron tail hat decoration. Still missing from the heist is the epaulette and its precious diamond, the Dresden White Stone. Not mentioned in any online reports are the finest works in the Green Vault Museum, the delicate ivory turnings described in the title poem of this volume. We can only hope they were never stolen in the first place and that art lovers can continue to view them on visits to the museum. We don't often benefit from the vagaries of the markets, but in this case we have. Go ahead, trade in the diamonds; leave us the human creativity.

# Acknowledgments

The author gratefully acknowledges the following journals for first publishing these poems:

*American Journal of Poetry*, "The Baptism of Christ in the Crowded Uffizi"; *Atlanta Review*, "Clarity"; *Beltway Poetry Quarterly*, "Deli with Sea Salt", "Slack Tide, Massey's Landing", "Choice"; *Cold Mountain Review*, "Goya's Black Paintings, Melville's White Whale"; *Confrontation*, "First Check"; *CONSEQUENCE*, "Old Soldier, Lower East Side"; *Constellations*, "Recalling Texas Rivers"; *december*, "Playground with Chain-Link Fence"; *Delmarva Review*, "Questions from the Museo Fran Daurel", "Leaving Spain", "The View from Heaven", "Leave Me a List", "Where Shells Come from"; *DMQ*, "The Denier" (also in *Blue Morning Light*); *Fourth River*, "In My Mind's Eye, in Baltimore"; *Free State Review*, "A Radiance"; *Gulf Stream*, "Van Gogh: Wheatfield and Starry Night"; *Innisfree Poetry Journal*, "Uncle Beale, a Baltimore Boy", "The Royal, the Whiskey, the Snow", "Ore Train, Early Morning"; *Iowa Review*, "States and Provinces"; *Nashville Review*, "A Room in the Prado", "What Goya Knew"; *New World Writing*, "A Meditation on the Land", "Your Fugitive Life", "Ghost Town Nocturne"; *North American Review*, "Around Phelps Lake"; *North Dakota Quarterly*, "An Old Man Who Believed in Math", "At the Automat"; *OneArt*, "New York", "Their World"; *Ploughshares*, "Mr. Levitz's X-Ray Machine"; *Poetry East*, "Night Train", "Savannah Channel"; *Potomac Review*, "The Celebration"; *Prairie Schooner*, "Blue Grass Poem"; *Pulsebeat*, "Eroica, 2022"; *Rosebud*, "Four Days at the Point"; *Saranac Review*, "At Swallow Falls"; *The Sextant Review*, "Loss–and the Green Vault Heist"; *Sundial*, "That Kind of Rain"; *Threepenny Review*, "Two Old People Starving"; *Valparaiso Poetry Review*, "Falling"

---

I'd like to thank the Director and Publisher of this series, Dr. Ross K. Tangedal; Executive Editor, Jeff Snowbarger; and press staff, especially editor Grace Dahl and her team, production director Chloe Verhelst, cover designer Brie O'Flyng, and media director Zoie Dinehart. This book has emerged and been helped along thanks to their good care. Also, thanks to friend and fellow writer William Heath for his support. I'm honored to have cover artwork provided by friend and very fine photographer Warren Simons.

Above all, this book is for Lily, Paul, and Barbara: "The strongest and sweetest songs yet remain to be sung" (Whitman).

DAVID SALNER'S writing has appeared in noted magazines including *Threepenny Review, Iowa Review, Prairie Schooner, Salmagundi, North American Review,* and *Ploughshares.* His novel, *A Place to Hide* (2021), won first place for historical fiction (1900s) from the Next Generation Indie Book Awards in 2022. Salner has been honored with grants from the Puffin Foundation, the Dr. Henry P. and Page Laughlin Fund, and two from the Maryland State Arts Council. He won the 2016 Lascaux Prize for Poetry and the Oboh Prize, and he has received nine Pushcart Prize nominations. He holds an MFA from the Iowa Writers' Workshop.

Salner has worked all over the country as iron ore miner, steelworker, machinist, bus driver, cab driver, garment laborer, longshoreman, teacher, and librarian. He was also an usher for minor league baseball. He lives in Millsboro, Delaware, with his wife, Barbara Greenway. He can be contacted at dsalner@hotmail.com and his website is: www.DSalner. wix.com/salner